M000031427

The Lazy Cook

Book 2: Quick And Easy Sweet Treats

Susie Kelly

blackbird

Blackbird Digital Books
London 2015
The moral right of the author has been asserted.
Cover artwork © David Lewis www.davidlewiscartoons.com
Cover design by Fena Lee www.pheeena.carbonmade.com
ISBN 9780993307058
All rights reserved. Except in the case of brief quotations quoted in reviews or critical articles, no part of this book may be used or reproduced in any manner whatsoever without written permission from the Publisher.
Any reliance the reader places on information in this book is strictly at their own risk. In no event will the publisher or author be liable for any loss or damage including without limitation, indirect or consequential loss or damage, or any loss or damage whatsoever in connection with the use of this book.

For Rob

Contents

Introduction

Whatever happened to cakes and desserts? When I was growing up we always had tea and biscuits mid-morning, a dessert after lunch, a piece of cake at tea-time, and a dessert after dinner. In fact no meal was complete without a sweet, even if it was nothing more than jelly and ice-cream. Goodness, seeing it like that it sounds as if we were forever eating, but none of our family or friends were overweight. Now we hardly ever have a sweet or cake unless we are entertaining. I wonder why? It must be all to do with the constant media obsession with weight and healthy eating I suppose.

I'm not suggesting that we should all be eating desserts twice a day, but it doesn't do any harm once in a while, does it? There are times when everybody deserves a little indulgence.

Most tiny villages in rural areas of France serve set-menu mid-day meals at very reasonable prices. It ensures that workers who may be away from home or far from the nearest town have somewhere to eat, because the French lunch is a sacrosanct ritual. There is no question of grabbing a sandwich and a plastic cup of coffee from a vending machine. *Quelle horreur!* It's about sitting down for a couple of hours with a small carafe of wine and working their way in a leisurely manner through a starter and main course, and sometimes a choice of either cheese or dessert. These meals offer excellent value, and we sometimes treat ourselves if we can find a menu that offers an alternative to meat. However, the desserts are often a terrible disappointment. Either a solitary piece of fresh fruit, or an ice-cream on a stick, or the commercially produced 'flan' – a slippery caramel custardy thing in a little aluminium pot. That's no good! I like a pudding to make me feel slightly guilty about eating it, but not enough to make me stop. :)

This collection is Part Two of my *Lazy Cook* Series and follows on from *The Lazy Cook (Book One): Quick And Easy Meatless Meals*. Both titles are the accumulation of decades of scribbled notes on backs of envelopes, tatty exercise books, recipes given to me by friends and vague recollections. I am always losing track of things, so I thought it was time to put everything in one place where I could find it quickly instead of hunting through drawers and cupboards. This is my personal collection of fail-safe quick and easy recipes for friends and family, which you are welcome to share. None of them require very much time or skill to prepare, and they make no claim to be haute cuisine, just wholesome recipes that anybody can follow.

There are numerous variations of most of them. I enjoy watching foodies and chefs giving a new twist to old favourites, and I enjoy trying them, but sometimes I think they go too far and the originals lose the identity that I loved in the first place. For me there's a great deal of nostalgia connected to the food we eat.

Except where specifically mentioned, the quantities given are not written in stone and do not require atomic precision. A little more or less of most ingredients won't make an enormous difference to the finished result. If there's an ingredient you don't like, then unless it is essential leave it out, or substitute something else. I'm one of those people who believe that fats are good for you, so I'm generous with them. You can always reduce the quantities to suit yourself.

I have indicated whether each recipe is vegan and/or gluten-free for the benefit of those who aren't certain, and have flagged up a 'raw egg' warning. It's quite disheartening when you think you have carefully prepared a meal for somebody with an intolerance or allergy, and discover at the last minute that you've accidentally included an ingredient that they can't eat. Of course, you can always substitute margarine or oil for butter in most recipes, although it will alter the taste somewhat.

To simplify measurements, I've converted Imperial and metric measurements wherever possible into cups and spoons. I find a set of stainless steel measuring cups and spoons, which are as cheap as chips and take up almost no space, more practical and quicker than weighing everything on kitchen scales – which I've found to my cost in the past to be not always reliable.

The volume of my measuring cup is 300 ml, equivalent to 10 US fluid ounces, or 10.5 Imperial fluid ounces – about the capacity of a normal teacup. Flours differ; egg sizes differ; oven temperatures differ; spoon sizes differ. What is under-seasoned for one person is too salty for another. If something doesn't turn out quite the way you hope, it's always worth having another go and tweaking the recipe to see if there's a solution.

1

Diets and Health Foods

Diets? I've tried them all. The Grapefruit Diet. The Coffee and Raw Egg Diet. The 5:2 Diet. The Cabbage Soup Diet. The High Protein Diet. The Raw Food Diet. The Low-Carb diet. Dukan. Atkins. Paleo. Boiled Egg. Ayds (I don't know if they still exist. They were mint-flavoured toffee-like things meant to suppress appetite. I ate the whole box in an afternoon). The Two-day Champagne Diet a model friend told me about: drink a glass or two of champagne for breakfast, again for lunch, and again for dinner. She told me you feel so good and dreamy you don't notice you haven't eaten and you can lose 5lbs or more. She was right; I felt like a princess and 'lost' 6lbs. Within a week I had found them again.

The diets all worked briefly but failed in the long term. Either they became boring, too time consuming, required ingredients that were difficult to find, were unreasonably expensive, or produced unpleasant and, in one case, dangerous side effects.

But most of all, the moment I began any diet that restricted any particular ingredient, I developed a craving for it. Although I don't have a very sweet tooth, if sugar, cakes, biscuits, chocolate were forbidden, I simply HAD to have them, and would gorge on them. If bread and pasta were out of bounds, I'd eat a whole baguette. Deprivation is a dirty word. I overheard someone discussing her diet with a friend: "I'm not allowed nuts, grains, sugar, dairy....." Not allowed! A bad choice of words, especially for anybody with a rebellious nature. The forbidden fruit is irresistible, so anything 'not allowed' is going to be a problem.

We live in an age where image is all-important and perfection means tall, slim, blonde, perfect skin, perfect teeth; and if it isn't perfect then there's always cosmetic surgery. Rubens and Botticelli didn't choose scrawny models; Marilyn Monroe was hardly skeletal. A 'comely wench' never did look like a stick insect. Yes, being grossly overweight is bad for health. But much depends upon metabolism as much as calories, and that's ultimately why diets don't work. Why not accept that that some of us will never squeeze into a size 10 again, but can be healthy, happy and glamorous as a size 14 upwards AND eat what we like? There's no denying that clothes look better on skinnies; but if you're not designed to be skinny, just be happy you have enough to eat. In fact too much to eat; that's the major cause of obesity. And the irony is that the slimming industry only exists because we live in a time where too many of us are able to afford to eat too much. Crazy or what?

We all know that too much fat isn't good for us, so I try to limit how much I eat and how often. However, if a recipe calls for butter, cream or cheese, I think it's a mistake to skimp on it, because you lose the deliciousness. Either use it to the full, or cook something different. I do not use low fat anything or any sugar substitutes.

What I have learned, finally, is that although I want to lose weight, equally as much I want to eat what I want, when I want. It's something I have thought over long and hard for years. While I want to be slimmer, I don't want to limit my meals to things I don't particularly enjoy, or follow some crazy eating plan that somebody has dreamed up.

So my philosophy is either worry endlessly about every mouthful, or just eat a little less, and exercise a little more. I don't want my final thought on earth to be: 'I wish I'd eaten more roast potatoes'.

2

Cold Desserts

The first eight recipes that follow were all given to me by my friend Abby, who kept house for an extremely demanding old lady who had her running about from dawn to dusk. Once a week she hosted a three-course bridge luncheon for which Abby had to cater, in between all her other tasks. All the old ladies loved their desserts, and Abby had a good collection, many from stately homes where other busy cooks had to whip things up in a hurry.

Yoghurt and marmalade
The bridge-playing ladies loved this crazily simple dessert that can be prepared in a great hurry. Stir together a tub of thick Greek yoghurt with two or three tablespoons of marmalade, either whole or strained to remove the rind. Any marmalade works. Seville gives quite a strong taste, while my preference is

for lime marmalade with a little fresh lime zest sprinkled over the top. Leave in the fridge for an hour.
Gluten free

Eton mess
Nothing to it! Just break up some meringues into small pieces (you can buy them but they're not difficult to make!), and stir into some whipped double cream with fresh strawberries, hulls removed and cut in half.
Gluten free

Raspberry whip
Sieve a 15oz tin of raspberries to remove any pips, and pour the liquid over 16 boudoir biscuits (lady fingers). Leave for 5-10 minutes for the biscuits to soak up the liquid, and then beat into a smooth purée. Fold in 1 cup of lightly whipped double cream, and divide between 4 glasses.

Chill for at least 2 hours before serving.

Ginger delight
This was a particular favourite with all the bridge-playing ladies.

You need a packet of ginger biscuits, ½ cup of coffee, a tablespoon of brandy and 1 cup of double cream.

Mix the coffee and brandy, bash the ginger biscuits in a plastic bag with a rolling pin to break them into large crumbs, then stir them into the coffee.

Whip the cream until thick, then stir in the coffee/biscuit mixture. Divide between 4 individual glasses and refrigerate overnight.

As a variation, you can replace the coffee and brandy with sherry. It did tend to make the old ladies nod off during their afternoon game.

The seductrice
No explanation for how this dessert got its name, but it is rather seductive!

Crush a packet of boudoir biscuits to fine crumbs (use a plastic bag and rolling pin). Beat them with the yolks of two eggs, ½ a pint of double cream, and a tablespoon of liqueur, such as Cointreau. Now whisk the two egg whites until stiff, fold into the mixture, pile into 4 glasses and chill well before serving.
Raw egg

Rich Russian dessert
Five minutes to make, plus an hour in the fridge, for this rich and delicious dessert.

Beat together 1 large egg and ¼ of a cup of soft brown sugar until thick. Stir in ½ a cup of raisins or sultanas, 2 cups of curd cheese, and the grated rind and juice of a large orange. Whip ½ a cup of double cream until it just holds its shape, and fold it into the mixture. Chill for at least an hour before serving and garnish with a few strands of orange zest.
*Gluten free *Raw egg**

Quick rich dessert
Beat together 4 egg yolks with ½ a cup of softened butter, then gradually beat in 1 cup of icing sugar and 1 tablespoon of rum. Stir in 1 cup of chopped walnuts, 1 cup of toasted hazelnuts and ½ a cup of glacé cherries. Pat into a rounded basin or a loaf tin lined with cling film, and refrigerate until set. Turn out and serve in slices, decorated with grated chocolate.
*Gluten free *Raw egg**

Gooseberry fool
Cook 4 cups of topped and tailed gooseberries with 1 tablespoon of caster sugar over a very low heat for 10 minutes.

Leave to cool, then mash to break them up. Whip ½ a cup of double cream, and fold in the fruit. Chill and serve very cold.

You can replace the gooseberries with any other fruit of your choice.

Gluten free

Speedy gula melaka (Japanese pearl pudding)
Does sago or tapioca ring an alarm bell? Does it take you back to school meals, sitting uncomfortably on a bench, shouted at to keep your elbows off the table and into your ribs, to sit up straight and not to talk?

Milk puddings were a frequent dessert at boarding school when I was there, and I was among the minority who enjoyed them. When others were moaning: "Oh NO! Frogspawn again!" I was licking my lips. I really loved rice pudding, semolina, sago or tapioca, with a dollop of jam, especially as it meant we wouldn't be having jelly with crinkly skin, or watery warm banana custard with brown bananas in it.

The French have a pretty name for tapioca: Japanese pearls. I think that's very apt, because once it has been cooked it does look like a collection of transparent pearls. Still, I know that some people just don't like the texture, so if you're one of them, just skip this recipe.

My first taste of gula melaka was in an Indonesian restaurant in London, where it was described on the menu as 'tapioca pudding'. I thought, it can't just be tapioca pudding. This was a high-end restaurant serving sophisticated and beautifully-presented food, so I ordered it out of curiosity.

Wow. I thought it was so delicious, especially after a spicy main course. Even though I'd eaten a large meal, I think I could have eaten a bucket of this dessert. It was cooling, soothing, rich, and slid down easily.

Abby's employer overheard us discussing the dessert one day, and became very excited. She'd enjoyed it in Singapore, and ordered Abby to find a recipe. Here is Abby's version.

You can use either sago or tapioca; they'll both give the same end result.

Bring 4 cups of water to the boil, add a pinch of salt, and pour, in a steady stream, 1 cup of tapioca or sago 'pearls'. Pour slowly and stir vigorously, otherwise they stick together and go lumpy. Simmer until transparent, 30-40 minutes, then strain in a fine colander and rinse with cold water.

Add ½ a cup of demerara sugar and ½ a cup of thick coconut cream, stirring to dissolve the cream, until you have a silky pale golden mixture. Cool thoroughly, and then refrigerate.

Dissolve 1 cup of brown sugar in ¼ of a cup of water. Don't stir, leave the syrup to cook over moderate heat until it starts to turn golden. Pour over the tapioca/sago mixture.

Serve chilled.
Vegan, gluten free

Cranachan
An adult and indulgent Scottish dessert that is quick and easy to make. Must be very healthy too, with all that oatmeal in it. :)

Spread half a cup of oatmeal in a heavy frying pan – cast iron is ideal. Put over a low heat, stirring frequently, until the oatmeal turns golden brown – don't let it burn – and leave to cool.

Whisk 1 cup of double cream until it begins to thicken, then fold in ¼ of a cup of runny honey and ¼ of a cup of Scotch whisky.

Put a couple of tablespoons of fresh or frozen raspberries in the bottom of 2 pretty glasses, stir a few tablespoons of the oatmeal into the cream and put a layer over the raspberries. Scatter the remaining oatmeal on top, and garnish with a few more raspberries. You can make this the night before.
Gluten-free if made with certified gluten-free oats

Passion fruit syllabub
It's funny how we take things for granted and don't value them when we have them in abundance, and then crave them when they are no longer readily available.

In my garden in Kenya I had two large avocado trees; the fruit used to fall on the ground and be left to rot. I rarely bothered to pick a mango from the tree, nor papaya, nor guavas with their beautiful pink flesh, nor the loquats which grew rampantly. Where once I could have picked them fresh, now all those fruits are only available as imported luxuries. Ho hum.

The entire garden was bordered by passion fruit vines, and of all the fruit I miss, I think passion fruit are my favourites. I love their sharp tangy flavour, and they go really well with cream in this simple, luscious sweet.

Cut 8 passion fruit in half and scrape out the flesh and seeds. Dissolve ½ a cup of sugar in ½ a cup of white wine and a tablespoon of lemon juice in a pan over gentle heat. Leave aside to cool to room temperature, and then beat with 1 cup of double cream into soft peaks. Fold in the passion fruit, pour into 4 glasses and chill to serve.
Gluten free

Fromage blanc
When I first came to live in France and tried this, I thought it was rather boring and not as tasty as yoghurt. It wasn't until I was offered it in a restaurant, sprinkled with sugar and a raspberry purée that I discovered that it's really rather good, and nothing could be easier to make. It's the ultimate instant dessert.*Gluten free*

Pear on sponge flan
My grandmother lived for many years in a bedsit with just a single ring gas cooker, so her creative cuisine options were very limited. I seem to remember we ate mostly tinned soups or eggs, but she always made an effort to produce a pudding, and this one can be made in 3 minutes.

You need a plain sponge flan (recipe in the Baking section) or buy one if you haven't time to make one. Take a tin of pears, plums, or mandarin oranges. Drain thoroughly. Put the sponge on a deep plate, and arrange the fruit on the sponge. Now pour over the contents of a small tin of evaporated milk, and grate over a little chocolate. Let it rest for about half an hour to allow the sponge to absorb any juice from the fruit, and the evaporated milk. Yummy!

Ginger toffee dessert
My lovely friend Sandy used to insist that she didn't like rich dishes full of cream, or anything that was 'mucked about with' but put a rich creamy dessert in front of her and she couldn't resist.

This sweet can be made well in advance and improves with keeping overnight. If you're entertaining, check that your guests like ginger, because not everybody does.

Boil a small unopened tin of condensed milk for 3 hours, or pressure cook it for 30 minutes, and then leave it until cold. The result will be a deliciously creamy pale brown toffee. Alternatively, if you're short of time, buy a jar of *dulce de leche*, or *confiture de lait*.

Take a packet of Marie biscuits and spread each with some of the toffee, then put a layer in the bottom of a glass bowl. On each biscuit put a thin slice of crystallised ginger, and dribble some of syrup over the top. Cover with a layer of whipped double cream.

Repeat the layers until the bowl is full, ending with a layer of cream. Decorate the top with slivers of ginger, and refrigerate overnight.

Sparkling fruit salad
On a hot summer day, a bowl of freshly chopped fruit with a dash of liqueur and a sprig of mint is a joy. Adding some bubbly into the mix makes it extra special.

Take a good mix of firm fruits – pineapple, melon, seedless grapes, lychees, and some berries – strawberries, raspberries, blueberries. Put them in a deep bowl with a couple of tablespoons of caster sugar and a dash of cognac, rum, Triple

Sec or Cointreau. Then pour over some sweet sparkling wine and leave to chill for 2-3 hours.
Vegan, gluten free

Avocado
While they're more usually eaten as a savoury, a friend who used to live in Zambia always ate hers sprinkled with lemon juice and sugar. Since I adore guacamole I was quite reluctant to risk ruining an avocado, but having tried it I really enjoyed it and still eat it that way quite often. If you fancy a try, you need a perfectly ripe avocado with no nasty brown bits in it. Peel it carefully, slice it thinly, sprinkle generously with the juice of a freshly-squeezed lemon or lime and a couple of teaspoons of sugar, and eat immediately.
Vegan, gluten free

Chocolate marquise
I'm not a chocaholic, but I recognise that for many people chocolate isn't just a treat, it's essential to their well-being and happiness, so I'm always happy to make this sumptuous dish. You need good quality chocolate for desserts, cheap chocolate doesn't taste nice. I use Lidl's own brand which is superb and very inexpensive.
Put ¾ of a cup of broken chocolate pieces in a bowl over a pan of hot water, and let it melt slowly. Don't let the water boil, and don't let the bowl touch the water.

Put 4 egg yolks in a bowl, beat them lightly and then pour on the melted chocolate, stirring well to blend. Add 2 tablespoons of Grand Marnier, Triple Sec or Cointreau and 2 tablespoons of brandy, and mix thoroughly.

Beat 4 egg whites to soft peaks with a pinch of salt, and fold in carefully to the chocolate mixture. Pour into 4 or 6 individual glasses and chill for a couple of hours.
Gluten free

Chocacado dessert

This comes from our lovely Australian friend, Don. It has a very firm texture and rich chocolate flavour, and makes a good alternative for anybody yearning for a rich chocolate dessert that does not contain dairy products or eggs.

(If you are making a vegan version, you need to check the ingredients on the chocolate wrapping to make sure it doesn't contain any milk products.)

Melt 1⅓ - 1½ cups of good quality chocolate in a bowl over a pan of hot water.

Blend 2 avocados with a good squeeze of lemon or lime juice and a teaspoon of vanilla extract. Add the melted chocolate and ¼ of a cup of icing sugar, and blend until smooth and creamy.

Either serve in very small pots or glasses – there's sufficient for 6-8 servings, or use to fill a crumb pie-shell. Refrigerate for 3 hours before serving. A few raspberries go very well with this, their acidity balances the extreme richness of the chocolate.
Vegan if using vegan chocolate (check ingredients), gluten free

Chocolate and lemon pudding

This is very rich, but at the same time quite light and the zing of the lemon means that it is not sickly.

Split 8 trifle sponges in half and use them to line a 2 pint bowl or loaf tin. You should have some pieces left; keep them to one side.

Put ½ of a cup of broken chocolate pieces into a bowl over a pan of hot water and leave to melt. Don't let the bowl touch the water.

Meanwhile cream ½ a cup of butter with ¾ of a cup of caster sugar, and then beat in 4 egg yolks, the grated rind and juice of one lemon, and the melted chocolate. It may look weird and curdled, but don't panic!

Whisk 4 egg whites until stiff and dry, and fold into the chocolate mixture.

Pour the mixture into the sponge-lined bowl, and lay the remaining sponge on top. Cover with a sheet of greaseproof paper or clingfilm, and then put a heavy weight on top. Leave overnight in the fridge.

To serve, turn out and cover with lightly whipped cream and a grating of chocolate.
Raw egg

Figs kahawa
My African cook used to make this for dessert after a large dinner when nobody felt like eating anything too rich. It will keep happily in the fridge for a couple of days, and only takes 5 minutes to prepare, so if you are going to be entertaining and are short on time, it can be made well in advance.

Allow 2-3 dried figs per person Snip off the hard little stalk, then put the figs in a saucepan and cover with water. Add a dessertspoon of instant coffee powder per 12 figs. (You can use decaf coffee.) Bring to the boil, then immediately remove from the heat. Leave aside for at least 8 hours, by which time the figs will have absorbed the coffee and plumped up. Chill and serve with single cream.
Vegan (omit the cream), gluten free

Poached pears kahawa
Kahawa is the Swahili word for coffee. This is an adaptation of the Figs Kahawa recipe and makes a nice and refreshing alternative to poached pears in red wine.

Peel the pears carefully, leaving the stalk. Place them upright in a pan, so that they are snuggled close together to stop them falling over. Now fill the pan with strong black coffee, sweetened according to taste. Bring to the boil, then reduce to a simmer and leave the pears to cook until you can stick a cocktail stick into them without it breaking. Remove the pears,

and continue to simmer the coffee until it is reduced to a thick syrup. Pour a little over each pear. Serve with cream.
Vegan (omit the cream), gluten free

Fragrant rice pudding
Just one of the limitless variations on the good old basic rice pudding. This is a summer recipe with a touch of oriental deliciousness.

It can be made on top of the stove, in a saucepan, with jasmine or basmati rice. However, I prefer the oven method, where the long, slow cooking produces a really luscious creamy pudding. Put ¼ of a cup of rice, ½ a cup of sugar, 3 cups of milk, ⅓ of a cup of rosewater, a tablespoon of butter and a tiny pinch of salt into an oven-proof dish and stir well. Bake in a very slow oven – 150C/300F – for 1½-2 hours, stirring every 20 minutes, until the rice is very tender and has absorbed all the liquid. Taste to see if you need to add a little more rosewater. Leave to cool, and refrigerate before serving. Decorate with chopped pistachio nuts.
Gluten free

Rice pudding with pears and raspberry
It sounds a strange affinity, lumpy rice and smooth pears, but this was regarded as a really luxurious dessert when I stayed with a school friend whose parents farmed 'up country' in Kenya, right out in the wilds and far from shops. I sometimes make it just for the pleasure of remembering time spent there. This pudding was their cook's speciality. He made the richest, creamiest rice pudding in the morning, and left it to cool all day. Just before serving he topped it with drained tinned pears which at the time were a luxury product, fresh being unobtainable – and topped it with a purée made from straining a tin of raspberries – another fruit unobtainable fresh. If you prefer to use fresh pears, peel and poach them until tender.
Gluten free

The evil malakoff

Here is another dessert that Sandy described as 'pure evil' because it is sheer luxury, loaded with cream, alcohol and sugar. A little does go a very long way, and it is best made the day before serving to give it time to really 'settle' and for the textures and tastes to blend.

Line a loaf tin with greased greaseproof paper. Put a layer of boudoir (ladyfinger) biscuits on the bottom of the tin and sprinkle with 2 tablespoons of orange-flavoured liqueur such as Triple-Sec, Grand Marnier or Cointreau. Use more boudoir biscuits to line all round the edges of the loaf tin.

Put a cupful of fresh raspberries over the biscuits on the bottom of the tin. Now cream together ½ a cup of softened butter and 3 tablespoons of caster sugar, stir in 3 tablespoons of ground almonds and fold in ¾ of a cup of lightly whipped double cream. Spread half of this mixture over the raspberries, and then cover with boudoir biscuits.

Sprinkle with 2 tablespoons of liqueur. Add another cup of raspberries, cover with the remaining cream mixture, and top that with a layer of boudoir biscuits sprinkled with another 2 tablespoons of liqueur.

Cover with greaseproof paper and put a weight on top. Refrigerate overnight and turn out just before serving. Cover with whipped cream, and garnish with some toasted almonds.

Variation: Substitute strawberries for the raspberries.

Key lime pie

So quick, so simple, so deliciously tart – how can anybody resist?

Make the base by crushing a dozen Digestive biscuits (Graham crackers) into fine crumbs, and mixing with 2 tablespoons of sugar and half a cup of melted butter. Line a pie dish with the mixture, pressing it down firmly.

In a large bowl empty one tin of **condensed** milk (not evaporated, which is runny, but condensed which is thick and sticky); add an equal quantity of double cream, and half the quantity of freshly squeezed or shop bought pure lime juice (not squash). If using fresh limes, add a teaspoon of grated zest. Stir together until the mixture begins to thicken, and pour over the crumb base. Refrigerate for at least six hours and serve very cold, decorated with a little grated zest or a sprinkle of biscuit crumbs.

Variation: If you have an ice-cream machine, scrape the whole chilled pie into it, add another cup of double cream, and churn until you achieve the required texture. Serve immediately.

Variation: For a firmer filling, substitute cream cheese for the double cream.

Lemon posset
I think by now all our friends must have eaten this with us, and asked for the recipe, which I had from an American lady, a reader, who invited me to lunch at her holiday home just outside Bordeaux. It's super quick and easy to make, as well as being wickedly indulgent.

Put 1½ cups of double (heavy) cream and 1 cup of sugar in a pan. Bring to the boil and allow to boil for 2-3 minutes. Watch it like a hawk, and keep the heat down low, otherwise it will boil over the moment you take your eyes off it. Remove from the heat and stir in 2½ tablespoons of fresh lemon juice (you can substitute orange or lime if you wish). Leave to cool for 10 minutes, then pour into 3-4 small serving dishes. It's very rich, so a little does go a long way. Leave to cool completely, then cover with cling film and refrigerate until set firm, about 4 hours. To serve, sprinkle with grated lemon zest, or a few fresh berries.
Gluten free

Lemon pavlova
I've always thought that before the advent of electricity, the thing I would have found most tiresome to make would be meringue. Having tried whisking eggs and sugar to the right

19

consistency by hand in the past, I'm eternally grateful for the electric whisk.

This recipe was given to me by my friend Sonia. It's an absolute dream, looks really impressive for a special occasion, and is far easier to make than the finished result might suggest. If I can do it, anybody can. It produces a lovely meringue that is crisp outside and slightly soft on the inside.

Set the oven to 170C/330F.

Put 4 egg whites in a very clean bowl, and whisk them until they are stiff. Then gradually whisk in 1 cup of caster sugar, no more than a tablespoon at a time, beating really well between each spoonful. Keep whisking until it's all shiny and stiff, and you could turn the bowl upside down without the contents falling out, and then stir in 1½ teaspoons of white vinegar, and 1½ teaspoons of cornflour (corn starch).
Spread it out on a sheet of greaseproof paper on an oven tray into a shape of your choice, round, square or rectangular. Try to make the edges higher than the centre. Put it in the pre-heated oven, and immediately lower the temperature to 150C/300F. Leave the meringue for an hour, just keeping an eye to see that it doesn't burn. If it starts to colour, lower the heat. After an hour, turn off the oven but leave the meringue in there until it's completely cold. Once it has cooled down remove it from the baking tray and place on a dish, sliding the greaseproof paper out from under it. That's the hard work done.

Now make the filling by stirring together 1 cup of **condensed** milk (not evaporated – shake the tin, if you can hear it sloshing around, it's not condensed) with 1 cup of lemon juice, either fresh or bottled, make sure it's pure juice and not syrup, and 1 cup of double cream. Stir it all together until it becomes thick and creamy, then spread it over the meringue.

Put it in the fridge for at least an hour, and just before serving decorate with thin slices of Kiwi fruit.
Gluten free

Ice creams

It's easy to make perfect ice cream without a machine, as I've been doing for 40 years.

For the basic ice cream, put 1½ cups of full-cream milk in a saucepan and bring to the boil. Then switch off. Beat 4 egg yolks with ⅔ cup of sugar, then add to the milk and reheat over medium until the sugar has dissolved, stirring, until the mixture begins to thicken slightly, just enough to leave a thin coating on the back of a spoon. You don't want it to be thick and gloopy, and if you let it boil you'll end up with scrambled eggs.

Leave aside until cold, then stir in 1½ cups of double cream and your chosen flavouring. Pour into a shallow plastic container and put into the freezer. Check after 1 hour, and it should be starting to freeze around the edges. Stir the frozen bits well into the rest with a fork, (or turn into a deep bowl and whisk) to break up the crystals and make the ice cream creamy. Repeat 3 times. The result isn't like Mr Whippy ice-cream, because it isn't full of air; it's quite firm, so take it out of the freezer and leave it to soften slightly for 30 minutes before serving.

That should give you six decent servings. Or four very large ones. :)
Gluten free

The flavour is only limited by your imagination, and you can experiment to find the strength of flavour that you personally like. These are a few of the flavours we and our friends enjoy:

Vanilla

For vanilla ice cream, put a vanilla pod in the pan with the milk and sugar, and leave it there until the milk is cold. Then remove the pod, wash and dry it, and put it in an airtight jar to use again. It gives a much nicer flavour than vanilla extract.
Gluten free

21

Earl Grey
Exactly as for vanilla, but replace the vanilla pod with two to four Earl Grey tea bags depending on how strong you want the flavour to be.
Gluten free

Coffee
According to how strong a coffee taste you want, dissolve instant coffee powder in the milk.
Gluten free

Brown bread
This was a popular ice cream in Victorian times. It has a rich caramel flavour and a slight crunchiness. Mix together ¾-1 cup of brown breadcrumbs and ½ a cup of brown sugar, and either grill or toast in a frying pan over low heat until the crumbs and sugar are deep brown and caramelised. Allow to cool, and then break up into small pieces and stir into the basic ice cream mixture.

Fruit
Add any fruit purée or syrup to to the basic mixture.
Gluten free

Chocolate
Melt 1 cup of chopped chocolate pieces and 1 tablespoon of chocolate powder in the milk.
Gluten free

Lavender
Add some fresh or dried lavender flowers to the milk before bringing it to the boil, and strain the flowers off once the milk has boiled and cooled. It's better to use less rather than more, because too many can produce an unpleasant medicinal taste. There should be just a tantalising and delicate hint of lavender. I use 1 heaped teaspoon of dried flowers to the basic quantity. Alternatively use lavender syrup.
Gluten free

Rose
This is another ice-cream that can be delicately flavoured with either rose water or rose syrup according to taste.
Gluten free

Violet
We love this flavour! Add either violet liqueur or violet syrup to the basic mix. Be cautious, the taste can be rather overpowering if you use too much.

Gingernut
Add crushed ginger biscuits to the basic mixture.

Kulfi (my favourite!)
To the basic mixture add a teaspoon of crushed cardamom seeds, and half a cup of chopped pistachio nuts.
Gluten free

3

Hot desserts

Old-fashioned bread and butter pudding

Dating back to the 'waste not, want not' era, this is a way of using up stale bread to make a nice comforting hot pudding.

Remove the crusts from 4 slices of white bread, spread with butter, and cut into quarters. Put a layer, butter side up, in a greased oven-proof dish. Sprinkle with a few raisins or sultanas. Repeat until all the bread is used up.

Dissolve 1 tablespoon of sugar in 1½ cups of milk over gentle heat. Let the milk cool to blood temperature, then whisk in 2 beaten eggs and ¼ of a teaspoon of vanilla essence. Pour over the bread through a strainer to catch any lumpy bits of egg, and leave for half an hour for the bread to soak up the liquid. Grate a little nutmeg over the top, and bake at 180C/350F until golden brown and set firm. Sprinkle with sugar and serve hot. Variation: replace the bread with slices of brioche.

Banana fritters

I don't often fry food, but this is a recipe that reminds me of Kenya, especially the coast where one of the hotels served the best fruit fritters I've ever eaten.

Mix 1 cup of plain flour with a beaten egg, 1½ tablespoons of caster sugar and sufficient water to make a thick batter.

Break 2-3 bananas into small pieces and add to the batter, stirring well.

Fry tablespoons of the mixture in hot oil until they are golden brown in colour, turning them to make sure they are cooked on all sides. Place them on kitchen paper, and serve immediately sprinkled with caster sugar and lemon juice.

Variations: replace the bananas with chunks of peeled apple, or pieces of pineapple.

Crumbles

The French have embraced the lovely English crumble and it's often seen on restaurant menus here now – and deservedly so! The marriage of soft fruit and crispy topping works so well and is an ideal dessert on a chilly day.

For apple crumble, peel, core and chop 4 large cooking apples. Sprinkle with lemon juice and put into an oven-proof dish. Stir in 2 tablespoons of sugar, ½ a teaspoon of cinnamon (optional) or half a dozen cloves (optional), the grated rind of a lemon, and a tablespoon of raisins (optional).

For rhubarb crumble, wash the rhubarb and cut into 1" (2 cm.) lengths. Put in an oven-proof dish with ½ a cup of sugar and a pinch of ginger.
For plum crumble, halve and stone the plums and put in the dish with 1-2 tablespoons of caster sugar and a tablespoon of water.

Make the crumble topping by processing or rubbing in by hand ½ a cup of butter into 1¼ cups of plain flour until it has the texture of large breadcrumbs. Stir in 1 cup of sugar and ½ a teaspoon of powdered ginger (optional). Mix it all together thoroughly, sprinkle over the chosen fruit and press down firmly. Bake at 200C/400F for 30-40 minutes, until the top is golden brown.

Serve hot, with single cream or evaporated milk.

Eve's pudding
A reminder of the parable of Eve successfully tempting Adam to eat the forbidden fruit in the garden of Eden, leading to their expulsion therefrom. Hmm. I'm not sure it was worth it for an apple, but still, this is a nice comforting dessert on a cold day.

Peel, core and chop two large cooking apples, and cook with 1 tablespoon of lemon juice and 2 tablespoons of water over a high heat for 5 minutes. Stir in 2 tablespoons of caster sugar and 1 heaped tablespoon of butter. Put into an ovenproof dish and leave to cool while you make the topping.

Cream ⅓ of a cup of butter with ⅔ of a cup of caster sugar. Beat 2 eggs, and add to the mixture a little at a time, alternating with 1 cup of self-raising flour. When all the egg and flour have been incorporated, add a pinch of salt and 1 tablespoon of boiling water, stirring well.

Pour over the apple mixture, and bake at 180C/350F for 30-35 minutes, until the top is firm and golden.

Serve hot, with single cream or evaporated milk.

4

Sweets (Candies)

Chocolate peanut butter fudge
Instead of serving a dessert when we entertain friends, we sometimes have a dish of dates, figs, crystallised fruit, nuts and sweets to nibble with our coffee. This is one of the most decadent sweets I know and disappears rapidly.

1 cup of whole milk
3 tablespoons of creamy peanut butter
3 cups of sugar
2 tablespoons of softened butter
2 tablespoon of cocoa powder

Put the peanut butter, sugar and milk into a large saucepan and whisk over moderate heat until the peanut butter has melted. Now increase the temperature slightly and bring the mixture to the boil, stirring from time to time to make sure it doesn't catch.

Meanwhile mash the butter with the cocoa powder into a smooth paste.

After 20 minutes, drop a small blob of the hot mixture onto a cold plate and prod it with your finger. It should form a smooth lump and slide around the plate. If it doesn't, continue cooking a little longer, until it does.

When you have the right texture, stir in the cocoa powder and butter and beat until the mixture loses its shiny appearance and becomes dull and grainy.

Pour it very quickly into a greased baking tin about 8" (20cm) square. It will start to set as soon as it comes off the heat, so don't hang around or it will end up setting in the saucepan.

When cool mark into squares. It would keep well in an airtight box in the fridge, but there's never any left over to keep.
Gluten free

Scottish tablet
This is another very special sweet treat, for which many thanks to my friend Hazel Robertson for sharing the recipe, which dates back to the early 18th century. A little goes a long way, and it's good served in small pieces for dessert. It is similar to fudge, but slightly firmer and more grainy, and should satisfy anybody with a sweet tooth.

The following quantity makes 4 pounds, so would be ideal for making as Christmas gifts.

Melt 1 cup of butter in 2 cups of water in a non-stick pan, then add 16 (yes - 16!) cups of icing sugar and bring to the boil, stirring constantly. When the mixture boils, add a 450gr tin of condensed milk, and boil for 20 minutes, stirring all the time to stop it sticking and burning.

Remove from the heat, and beat the mixture well for 5 minutes, then add the flavouring of your choice – vanilla, coffee essence, chopped nuts, or for a very adult taste, a slug of whisky. Pour into a buttered rectangular pan, and once cool cut into slices about 3" x 2" (8 cm. x 5cm).

When it is quite cold, wrap in non-stick paper and keep in an airtight container.
Gluten free

5

Baking

Warning! If you are a cupcake-lover, please look away now.

At the risk of becoming a global hate figure and being demonised, I have to say that I think they are absolutely horrible little things, and a rip-off. There, I've said it!

Of course they look beautiful, and I can imagine the pleasure that people get from producing works of art in sugar, but eek, the thought of eating all that sickly sweetness, often more topping than actual cake, really doesn't appeal. Having to lick your way through a mountain of frosting to get to the sponge just seems wrong, wrong, wrong!

But mention butterfly cakes, and I'm in heaven, five years old, back in our kitchen in south-west London. My mother is baking. Her left arm is cradling a classic earthenware mixing bowl – creamy brown on the outside, with a raised pattern – and white inside. With her right hand she's vigorously beating butter and sugar with a large wooden spoon. Meantime I'm placing little crinkly waxed paper cups into a baking tin. When the butter and sugar are creamy, in goes the flour, followed by beaten egg and milk. My mother carefully divides the mixture equally into the paper cups, and puts the tin in the oven.

Now for the best part, the part I've been waiting for. Scraping out the bowl and eating the raw mixture. Every tiny little spot and drop, until the bowl is empty and the spoon has been licked clean. Why bother cooking it when the mixture is so delicious?

The little cakes come out of the oven and set aside to cool on a wire rack, the aroma is mouth-watering.

More butter goes into the washed mixing bowl, and my mother beats it until it is soft, and then starts mixing in icing sugar, a little at a time. Then she adds the juice from a freshly-squeezed lemon, drop by drop, until the mixture is thick and smooth and creamy.

Once the cakes are quite cold, she slices off the tops, which she cuts in half. She divides the lemon butter cream between the cakes, spreading it over the top. And now it's my turn to place the halves of the tops so that they stick up in the butter cream, turning the little sponges into butterfly cakes.

My reward is another go at licking the spoon and cleaning out the bowl of lemon butter cream. The sponge is moist, the balance of the butter cream is perfect, and the lemon juice gives a lovely fresh tang. You can keep all the cupcakes you want, just leave the butterfly cakes for me, please.

Butterfly cakes

I make my basic sponge mixture slightly differently from the way my mother did, because I'm lazy and you don't have to cream the butter.

Preheat the oven to 190C/375F. Grease a dozen fluted cupcake cases with melted butter using a pastry brush. Stand them in a cupcake baking tin.

Mix together a scant cup of plain flour, a scant ½ cup of caster sugar, 1 teaspoon of baking powder and 2 beaten eggs.

31

Melt 2 rounded tablespoons of butter over gentle heat, leave to cool for 10 minutes, then stir into the other ingredients and mix well. Divide between the paper cases.

Bake for 10 minutes until golden and risen. Stick a wooden cocktail stick through the centre to check for doneness – it should come out clean.

Leave the cakes to cool while you decide how to decorate them.

If you're making butterfly cakes, the recipe for lemon butter cream is to gradually beat 2 cups of sifted icing sugar with ½ a cup of softened butter and then add 2 tablespoons of lemon juice, and the finely grated rind of one lemon.

If you're going the cupcake route, then you'll know what to do. :)

Singing hinny
This is a great recipe when friends drop by at short notice for a cup of tea or coffee, because it can be made very quickly on the stove top, no need to heat the oven. Oh, and because it tastes wonderful. Its name comes from the fact that when it is cooking, the sultanas 'sing' – wouldn't we all if we were trapped on a red hot griddle! It's similar to a large slightly flat scone, but easier to make, less temperamental and you don't need to use the oven.

If you have a processor, put in 3 cups of plain flour, a pinch of salt, ½ a teaspoon of bicarbonate of soda, 1 teaspoon of cream of tartar, then add ⅓ of a cup of butter and process into a thick crumb. Otherwise rub the fat in by hand. Add ¾ of a cup of currants or sultanas and sufficient milk – about ¾ of a cup, to make a firm dough. Turn onto a floured board and pat into a round about ½" (1 cm.) thick.
Heat a large heavy frying pan or griddle, and sprinkle it with flour. Lay the dough on it, and let it cook over gentle heat for about 5 minutes. Keep the heat low to avoid burning the fruit.

Turn over and cook on the other side for another 5 minutes. Listen to the singing of the hinny.

Once cooked, leave to cool on a wire rack for 15 minutes, then cut into eighths, split each piece and butter. Serve immediately.

Sponge flan

An easy bake, and useful as either a cake or dessert base, covered with fruit and whipped cream. My old sponge flan baking tin was a nightmare as it had a deep curved 'gutter' around the outer part, and was virtually impossible to stop the sponge sticking at some point no matter how well it was greased and floured. The newer version makes it much easier. It's just a round non-stick cake tin with fluted sloping sides.

For an 8" (20 cm.) flan beat 3 eggs with 6 tablespoons of caster sugar until it forms a thick pale mixture. Carefully, gently, fold in 6 tablespoons of sifted plain flour and a pinch of salt until you can't see any more flour.

Although my flan tin is non-stick, I still brush it with melted butter and shake some flour into it before baking at 220C/425F for 10 minutes, when it should bounce back if you prod it with a finger. Not too hard, you don't want to make a hole in it.

Highland Scottish shortbread biscuits

Another recipe from Hazel Robertson, queen of cakes and cookies.

Beat together 2 cups of softened butter and 1½ cups of icing sugar and then gradually beat in 5 cups of plain flour. For crispier biscuits, replace ¼ of a cup of flour with ¼ of a cup of cornflour

Knead lightly with your hands, then leave to rest for 15 minutes.

Divide the mixture into 4, sprinkle the work surface with brown sugar, and roll the mixture out into sausage shapes. Roll the 'sausages' into the diameter you want for the finished biscuits. Cut with a very sharp knife into thin slices. You can freeze now to cook later, or cook straight away.

Cover a baking tray with non-stick paper and put the biscuits on it, leaving ample space between them as they will spread. Bake at 160C/325F until the biscuits are a delicate golden brown – about 30 minutes depending on the thickness. Remove from the oven and leave to cool for a few moments, then transfer to a wire rack until quite cold. Keep in a sealed box.

Flapjacks
As far as I know, there is no perfect substitute for Golden Syrup, so if you are unable to find it you could experiment with honey, corn syrup, agave syrup if you want to, but none of them will give the same result.
Heat ½ a cup of sugar, ¾ of a cup butter and 1 tablespoon of Golden Syrup together in a pan over medium heat until the butter has melted, and then remove from the heat and stir in 1 cup of rolled oats.

Line a shallow 7-8" (18-20 cm) square or rectangular cake tin with greaseproof paper and press the mixture down very firmly over the base.

For chewy flapjacks, preheat the oven to 175C/350F, and bake for 25-30 minutes.
For crispy flapjacks, preheat the oven to 190C/375F and bake for 25-30 minutes.

Allow to cool in the tin for 10 minutes before cutting into squares or bars. Leave until cold then remove from the tin.

Peanut butter criss-cross cookies
Apart from being so easy to make – ideal for very young children who like to cook, these are gluten-free. When my children were very young they could demolish a heap of these faster than the eye could see.

Beat 1 cup of peanut butter with ⅓ of a cup of sugar, 1 egg and a drop of vanilla essence. Take teaspoon-sized chunks of the mixture and roll into walnut-sized balls with your hands. Put them on a greased baking sheet, leaving room for them to spread, and then flatten them with the back of a fork to print a criss-cross pattern on them.

Bake at 180C/350F for about 20 minutes, and leave on the baking tray until cool.
Vegan, gluten free

Scotch pancakes or drop scones
Lovely little things, so quick and easy to make for a breakfast or teatime treat.

Sift together 4 cups of plain flour, 2 teaspoons of bicarbonate of soda, 3 teaspoons of cream of tartar and a pinch of salt. Beat 2 eggs with 4 tablespoons of caster sugar and a cup of milk and add to the mixture, adding more milk until you have a consistency like double cream.

Heat a cast iron frying pan or griddle over medium heat, grease lightly with a small amount of butter. Drop tablespoons of the batter onto the pan. After a couple of minutes holes will begin to appear on the surface, which means it's time to flip the pancakes over onto the other side for a minute or so, until both sides are golden. Keep the pancakes covered with a clean cloth until you have used all the batter.

Serve with butter, jam, golden syrup or maple syrup.

Ginger shortcake
Melt-in-the-mouth shortbread topped with a luscious ginger icing.

Cream ¾ of a cup of butter with ⅓ of a cup of caster sugar. Stir in 1½ cups of self-raising flour and 1 teaspoon of powdered ginger.

Press into a greased 7" (18 cm.) sandwich tin and bake at 160C/325F for 40 minutes.

Meantime melt together ½ a cup of icing sugar, ⅓ of a cup of butter, 1 teaspoon of ginger and 1 tablespoon of Golden Syrup.

When the shortbread is cooked, pour the icing over and leave in the tin until cold and set. Cut into squares, and store in an airtight box.

Cherry crinkles
Delicate, lacy little biscuits that are easy to make and even easier to eat.

Mix together ½ a cup of chopped almonds or walnuts and ⅓ of a cup of glacé cherries. Cream together ¼ of a cup of butter and ⅓ of a cup of sugar, then add the fruit, nuts and ¼ of a cup plain flour.

Put teaspoonfuls of the mixture onto a greased baking sheet, leaving plenty of room between them because they will spread.

Bake at 180C/350F for 7-8 minutes, until golden brown. Let them cool on the baking sheet for a few minutes, then put on a wire rack.

If you don't mind getting messy, you can melt some chocolate and spread it on the underside of the crinkles, like florentines. I prefer them without.

Pip's cake
When we rented out our 2 little gîtes as holiday homes, a dear little boy called Pip liked to come round to cook in our kitchen. He said his Mummy didn't want him messing up the kitchen in their cottage, so he came to mess up mine instead. One of the things he showed me to make was this cake. He was just seven. It turned out perfectly, really nice and moist.

In a large mixing bowl put 1½ cups of sugar, 2 eggs, ½ tsp salt, 2 cups of flour, 2 teaspoons of bicarbonate of soda and 2 cups of tinned fruit cocktail, drained. Keep the syrup aside in case of need.

If necessary add a little of the syrup to give the mixture a dropping texture. Spread it carefully – we took a LONG time to do this :) – into a cake tin about 9" x 6" (22 x 15 cm.) lined with greased greaseproof paper.

Over the top of the mixture scatter half a cup of chopped nuts. Bake at 180C/350F for 40-60 minutes, until firm to the touch. Leave to cool in tin, and then turn out.

(Pip reminded me that you can cut yourself very badly on tins, so you must be extremely careful and always ask an adult to open them for you. Also make sure your saucepan handles do not overhang the side of the hob where little children could pull them down and burn themselves. If you drop grease on the floor, wipe it up straight away so that you don't skid and fall over. And always ask an adult to put things in and take them out of a hot oven. He was a very sensible and safety-conscious little boy.)

Pot-sponge cake

A local French farmer's wife gave me this recipe. It's really quick to make, doesn't taste of olive oil, and seems to work every time. Combine 1 pot of plain yoghurt, 1 pot of olive oil, 2 pots of self-raising flour, one pot of sugar, 2 eggs, and a teaspoon of baking powder. Add sufficient milk to make a soft dropping mixture. Bake at 180C/350F in a 9" (22 cm) diameter lined cake tin for about 35 minutes, until it springs back when prodded with a finger.

Scones

This is my friend Hazel's recipe for scones, another quick and easy teatime treat. If you follow her directions, you'll have scones to be proud of.

Turn oven to 250C/475F.

Rub ½ a cup of butter into 2 scant cups of self-raising flour, with fingers or in a food processor, until it resembles fine breadcrumbs. Add a pinch of salt and ½ a teaspoon of bicarbonate of soda, and sufficient milk or buttermilk to make a firm dough.

Gently roll out the dough (handle as lightly as possible) to a depth of about ¾" (1.5 cm), then cut into 2" (5 cm) circles. Brush with a little milk and sprinkle with a little grated cheese for savoury scones, or sugar for sweet scones. Bake for 12-15 minutes.

For cheese scones, add ½ a cup of strong grated cheese and ¼ of a teaspoon of mustard.

For herb scones, add 1 soup spoon of chopped chives.

For sweet scones, add 2 soup spoons of sugar before adding the milk. Best eaten with clotted cream and jam.

For fruit scones: add just under ½ a cup of sugar, and ½ a cup of raisins.

6

Drinks

Cafe brulot
To warm you up on a cold wintery day.

Put ¾ of a cup of brandy, 6 sugar lumps, a slice of orange peel, 6 whole cloves and a small stick of cinnamon in a shallow pan. Bring to the boil and then flambée by tilting the pan onto the flame, or lighting with a match. Slowly add three cups of hot strong coffee, and serve immediately in small cups.
Vegan, gluten free

Atholl brose
When I was an 18-year-old secretary in Kenya, a very kind elderly Scottish Presbyterian couple invited me to their house for New Year's Eve. My boss and his wife were also amongst the guests. The house servant circulated with trays of a luscious creamy drink that I kept knocking back. And that's all I remember. I awoke late afternoon the next day, at my boss's

house, feeling bewildered, in one of the spare rooms that seemed to be tilting like a small boat on a wild sea. The only way to stop the boat rocking was to close my eyes.

I learned that I had climbed onto a table and started singing *Malaika*, a popular African song, while trying to take off all my clothes. I had no recollection at all. And that was my first introduction to atholl brose, which left a lasting impression, despite which I still love this drink.

The mixture of oatmeal, honey, whisky and cream blends perfectly: the silkiness of the oat water, the richness of the cream, the kick of the whisky and the sweetness of the honey. You can adjust any of the ingredients to find the combination that works best for you.

Put 2 cups of oatmeal in six cups of water, and leave to stand overnight. Pass through a fine strainer, keeping the liquid which will have become a silky water, and discarding the oatmeal. Stir in 2 cups of single cream, ½ a cup of whisky and 2 tablespoons of runny honey. Mix well, and serve cold.

Lemon barley water
A refreshing cold drink.

Put ⅓ of a cup of pearl barley and 1 cup of sugar into a large jar.

Add the grated rind and the juice of two lemons.

Add 8 cups of boiling water.

Leave to stand in a very cool place until quite cold. Pour into clean, sterilised bottles and keep in a cool, dark place.
Vegan

Egg nog
When you feel in need of a pick-me-up, if you're cold, lonely, sad or just want a cuddle in a glass, egg nog could be the answer.

Heat 1 cup of double cream with one cup of milk, (or two cups of milk for a less rich version), ¼ of a cup of sugar and a generous pinch of nutmeg, until the surface begins to tremble. Don't let it boil.

Blend 2 fresh eggs until thick and creamy, and add the hot mixture keeping the blender running all the time until the mixture is thick and frothy.

Finally, (and optionally) add a tot of your choice of alcohol – brandy, Cognac or rum. Wrap your hands around the warm glass; have a good sniff, and then sip the contents with your eyes closed so that nothing distracts you from the moment.
Serves 2.
Gluten free

Cold creamed coffee
To cool you down on a hot summery day.

To a pint of boiling coffee add a teaspoon of powdered cinnamon. Let it cool completely. Once cool, add a dash of brandy and a couple of tablespoons of single cream. Chill thoroughly and serve very cold.
Gluten free

Elderflower cordial
We are lucky to have plenty of elder trees near us, and most years I make half a gallon of this wonderfully refreshing summer drink, and freeze it in bottles so that it lasts until the following year.

Thoroughly rinse 25 elder flower heads (not the little tiny flowers, but the large bunches.). Put them in a very clean bucket with 4 chopped whole oranges, 1 chopped whole lemon,

6 cups of caster sugar, 2 tablespoons of tartaric acid which you can buy from a pharmacy, and 8 cups of cold water.

Cover with a clean cloth, and leave for 48 hours, stirring from time to time.

Strain into clean bottles and refrigerate or freeze. Dilute to taste.
Vegan, gluten free

7

Titbits

Baking tin size conversions
I often find that a recipe calls for size and shape of tin that I don't have. The following table shows you how to substitute square for round tins, and vice versa.

Round size	Square size
8" (20 cm)	7" (18 cm)
9" (23 cm)	8" (20 cm)
10" (25 cm)	9" (23 cm)
11" (28 cm)	10" (25 cm)
12" (30 cm)	11" (28 cm)

DIY baking powder/self-raising flour
If you run out of baking powder, make your own by combining 1 teaspoon of cream of tartar and ½ a teaspoon of bicarbonate of soda. This provides the equivalent of one teaspoon of baking powder. If you need a larger quantity, just remember the ratio of cream of tartar to bicarbonate of soda is 2:1. It's best used straight away.

To make self-raising flour, add one teaspoon of baking powder (or equivalent homemade) and a pinch of salt to 1 cup of plain flour.

Ginger
Root ginger freezes and keeps very well if you wrap it in kitchen foil, and is very easy to grate when frozen. If you wash the skin first, and dry it, you can grate the whole root without peeling, or easily scrape the skin off with a knife.

Lemons
Lemons also freeze and keep really well, wrapped in kitchen foil. Wash and dry them carefully before freezing. You can then grate them – all of them, rind, pith and flesh to enliven a salad or fish dish, and they produce copious amounts of juice after they've been frozen. I buy them when they're cheap and keep a good stock in the freezer.

Handling pastry
If you are lining a pie dish or flan case with delicate pastry, roll it out first onto greaseproof paper and lift it into place on the paper. Trim the paper and leave it in the dish while you bake the pastry.

Peeling Kiwi fruit
I find peeling off the fuzzy skin a bit messy, but there's an easier way.

Cut both ends off, then slide a narrow dessert spoon with a sharp edge between the skin and the fruit and run it all the way around. This should leave the fruit intact and perfectly peeled.

Skinning mango
In Kenya we always cut both the sides of a mango, scored it across in two directions and then pushed the skin upwards, forming something that looked like a hedgehog, and chewed the resulting cubes flesh off. It left you with a sticky face.

Instead of making a 'hedgehog', slice off both the sides of the mango as close to the seed as possible, then using a large serving spoon push it from the bottom to the top between the peel and the skin to remove the peel in one smooth movement.

Eggs
If you are breaking a number of eggs into a bowl and don't first break them individually into a cup, one day you WILL come across a bad one and spoil the rest.

If you tap eggs on a flat surface rather than a sharp edge the shells are less likely to splinter.

You can substitute various ingredients for eggs when baking – including, amongst others, flax seeds, oil, banana and even snow. Personally I find that apple sauce works best, ¼ of a cup in place of 1 egg.

SUSIE KELLY

Born a Londoner, Susie Kelly spent most of the first 25 years of her life in Kenya, and now lives in south-west France with her husband and assorted animals. She's slightly scatterbrained and believes that compassion, courage and a sense of humour are the three essentials for surviving life in the 21st century. She gets on best with animals, eccentrics, and elderly people.

CONNECT WITH SUSIE

Blog:
http://nodamnblog.wordpress.com

Facebook:
https://www.facebook.com/people/Susie-Kelly/Author

Twitter:
@SusieEnFrance

Sign up to the Susie Kelly Mailing List
http://eepurl.com/zyBFP
(Securely managed by Mailchimp, details are never, ever shared)

PICTURE CREDITS

C1 Cartoon woman
ID 28220755 © Djembe | Dreamstime.com
C2 Ice coffee with whipped cream
ID 25480681 © Nikoleta Vukovic || Dreamstime.com
C3 Crumble
Creative Commons freefoodphotos.com
C4 Homemade Chocolate Fudge
ID 6608939 © Helen Shorey | Dreamstime.com
C5 Baking ingredients
ID 28248628 © Jminso679 | Dreamstime.com
C6 Elderflower Cordial Creative Commons 2.0 Generic Magda
from Wakefield / Leeds, UK

MORE BOOKS BY SUSIE KELLY

The Lazy Cook (Book One): Quick And Easy Meatless Meals
(June 2015, Blackbird) The first of Susie's delightful round-ups
of her favourite quick, simple, easy recipes, sprinkled with
anecdote and humour.

*Travels With Tinkerbelle: 6,000 Miles Around France In A
Mechanical Wreck* (Blackbird 2012) Join Susie, husband Terry
and their two dogs on a camping trip around the circumference
of France.

*The Valley of Heaven and Hell: Cycling in the Shadow of
Marie-Antoinette* (Blackbird 2011) Novice cyclist Susie bikes
500 miles through Paris and Versailles, the battlefields of
World War 1, the Champagne region and more. Ebook &
paperback.

Two Steps Backward (Bantam 2004) The trials and tribulations
of moving a family and many animals from the UK to a run-
down smallholding in SW France. Paperback.

I Wish I Could Say I Was Sorry (Blackbird 2013)
With her usual humour and honesty, Susie recalls a 1950s
childhood in post-war London's every shade of grey which
contrasts vividly with the splendours of Africa. A moving and
often shocking insight in to the earlier life of the bestselling
travel writer.

*Swallows & Robins:The Laughs & Tears Of A Holiday Home
Owner* (Blackbird 2012) 'Laugh out loud funny and a must
read for anyone dreaming of the good life running gites in
France.' The Good Life France

Best Foot Forward: A 500-Mile Walk Through Hidden France (Transworld 2000/Blackbird 2011) A touching and inspiring tale of the Texan pioneering spirit, English eccentricity, and two women old enough to know better.

If you loved this book and would like to know more about becoming a **Reader Ambassador** for *The Lazy Cook*, please email us at blackbird.digibooks@gmail.com and we'll let you know how you can become a valuable, visible, part of this book's journey to a wider audience.

MORE BLACKBIRD DIGITAL BOOKS

The Dream Theatre by Sarah Ball (2011)
The Widow's To Do List by Stephanie Zia (2012)
A London Steal by Elle Ford (2012)
Cats Through History by Christina Hamilton (2013)
On Foot Across France by Tim Salmon (2013)
That Special Someone by Tanya Bullock (2014)
The Road To Donetsk by Diane Chandler (2015)
The Modigliani Girl by Jacqui Lofthouse (2015)
Love & Justice by Diana Morgan-Hill (2015)

Blackbird Digital Books

A publishing company for the digital age

We publish rights-reverted and new titles by established quality
writers alongside exciting new talent.

Email: blackbird.digibooks@gmail.com
http://blackbird-books.com
@blackbirdebooks

READER AMBASSADORS

1. Frank Hubeny

2. Jacqui Brown, French Village Diaries

3. Hazel Hatswell

4. Susan Keefe

Made in the USA
Middletown, DE
24 February 2020

85264198R00038